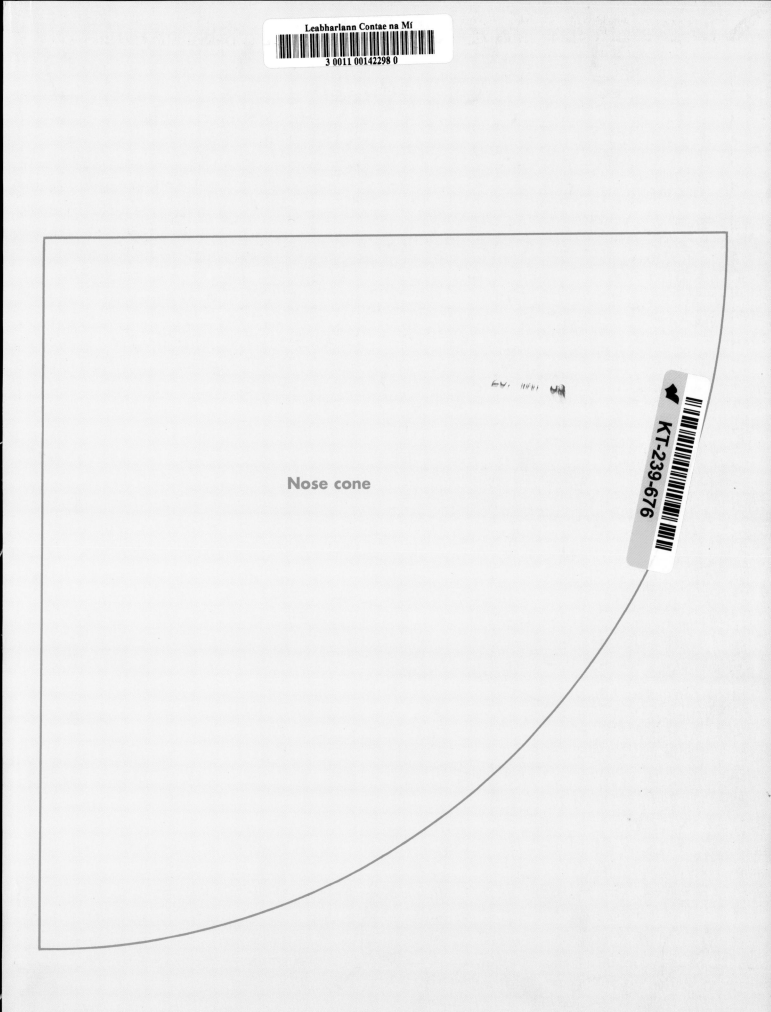

Nose cone

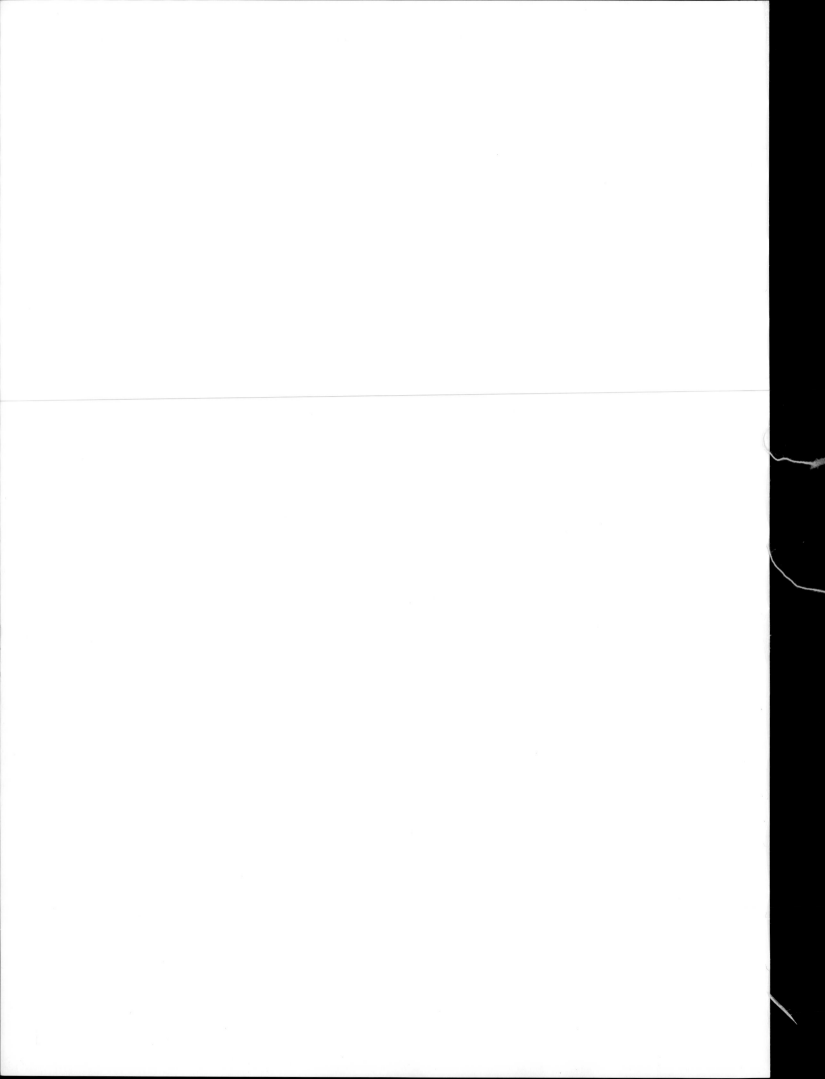

HOW SCIENCE WORKS
ROCKETS
AND OTHER SPACECRAFT

JOHN FARNDON

ALADDIN/WATTS
LONDON • SYDNEY

CONTENTS

INTRODUCTION

The rockets that launch spacecraft into space are huge and powerful. Yet they work in much the same way as fireworks. Both get their power by burning fuels. As they burn, hot gases push out of the back of the rocket. This drives the rocket forwards.

This book tells you about all kinds of rockets and spacecraft. It also reveals how the astronauts that fly them cope with life in space. Some chapters come with a project. If you do all of them, you can build a rocket that soars high into the sky.

To make the projects, you will need: a plastic bottle, paper, card, balsa wood, a craft knife, a drill, scissors, craft glue, a strong epoxy glue, a ruler, a pencil, oil-based paints, tin foil, a cork, and a bicycle pump and valve.

Rocket project box

Science experiment project box

© Aladdin Books Ltd 2000

Designed and produced by
Aladdin Books Ltd
28 Percy Street
London W1P 0LD

First published in
Great Britain in 2000 by
Franklin Watts
96 Leonard Street
London EC2A 4XD

ISBN 0 7496 3864 8

A catalogue record for this book is available from the British Library.

Printed in Belgium
All rights reserved

Editor
Jim Pipe

Science Consultant
Bryson Gore

Series Design
David West Children's Books

Designer
Simon Morse

Illustrators
Ian Thompson, Catherine Ward,
Don Simpson – Specs Art,
Simon Tegg, Graham White,
Alex Pang, Francis Phillipps,
Simon Bishop and
Richard Rockwood

Picture Research
Brooks Krikler Research

THE SCIENCE OF SPACE

Huge teams of scientists are needed to develop the technology to send spacecraft into space. They have to build powerful rockets to lift the spacecraft above the Earth against the pull of Earth's gravity.

Once in space, some spacecraft are controlled automatically from the ground. Others have a crew, and the spacecraft must be built to carry them safely.

Rocket fuels burn so fiercely that rockets must be built from special materials. See more on page 14.

Nose cone

CONTROLS

There are no wheels to steer with in space. Instead, spacecraft are guided by small "booster" rockets on the side. These are turned to push the spacecraft in the right direction.

Satellite

Outer shell

Mir space station

Space shuttle

LIVING IN SPACE

Once in space, the crew are out on their own. The spacecraft must provide all their needs and protect them from dangerous radiation. In space, the spacecraft is free of the pull of gravity which holds things down on the ground. This makes even showering tricky!

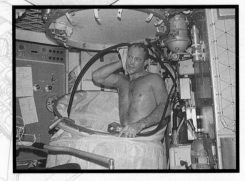

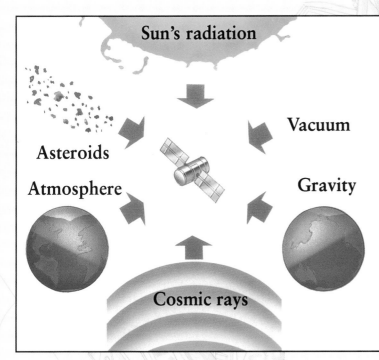

Sun's radiation

Vacuum

Asteroids

Atmosphere

Gravity

Cosmic rays

WHAT IS SPACE?

Rocket scientists have to think about what space is like. Gravity and Earth's atmosphere still affect a spacecraft when it is in orbit, but the vacuum that exists in space creates other problems, too.

Harmful rays from the Sun and the rest of the universe can also damage a spacecraft, as can even tiny pieces of floating rock.

Venera

Lunar module

CONSTRUCTION

Most rockets are quite similar, but the small spacecraft they carry vary enormously. Venera was made to visit Venus. The lunar probe was designed for an unmanned visit to the Moon. The lunar module was designed to land astronauts on the Moon's surface. Learn more about spacecraft on page 22.

Fuel tanks

Lunar probe

The spacecraft takes off as soon as the main rocket motors are fired. This is a dangerous time and during the final countdown to "lift-off" the area around the rocket is completely cleared. Turn to page 10 to learn about rocket power.

Burner where the fuels burn

CHAPTER 1 – INTO SPACE

One of the hardest things for spacecraft to do is to actually get off the ground. To climb into space, a spacecraft needs to overcome gravity, the force of attraction  that holds everything on the ground. So far, the only way scientists have found of doing this is to use huge rockets to thrust spacecraft upwards against gravity.

Break out! If a rocket is launched with enough power, it can break free of Earth's gravity.

When you hold a grapefruit and a tennis ball (*above*), the different weights that you feel are the force of Earth's gravity pulling on their two different masses.

Mass and Weight

Fill a balloon with water and it feels very heavy. Now lower the balloon into water. You will see that it feels much lighter. This is because the pressure of the outside water is lifting it up.

Weight is a measure of the pull of gravity, and it can change. This is why scientists talk about "mass". This is the amount of matter in an object. It's the same wherever you measure it.

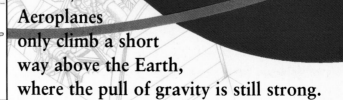

Aeroplanes only climb a short way above the Earth, where the pull of gravity is still strong.

GRAVITY

Gravity doesn't only hold things on the ground. It is the force of attraction between every bit of matter in the universe. It is the force which makes the Earth and all the other planets stay close to the Sun and stay circling around it.

Sun

Moon

The Moon stays in orbit (circling the Earth) because it and the Earth are pulled together by each other's gravity.

Satellites stay up because they are moving too fast to fall. Their speed balances out the pull of Earth's gravity.

Gravity gets weaker higher up, so a satellite circling the Earth low down has to travel much faster to stay up.

LOSING WEIGHT

Astronauts in spacecraft orbiting the Earth float around freely as if they were weightless. This is because the spacecraft is whizzing around the Earth so fast that a force called centrifugal force balances the effect of gravity. Astronauts practise being weightless by flying in a plane that falls so fast that they float off the floor (*top*).

FORCES NEEDED

Aeroplanes use the pressure of air on their wings to lift them up. But there is no air far above the Earth and wings would be useless.

So rocket motors alone must develop enough "thrust" or push to overcome the spacecraft's weight.

The British scientist Sir Isaac Newton (1642–1727) discovered many of the laws about momentum. Momentum is what keeps a moving object going in a straight line unless a force acts on it.

TYPES OF ENERGY

Energy comes in two forms. Potential energy (PE) is energy stored up ready for action, like the unburned fuel in a rocket.

Kinetic energy (KE) is the energy something has because it's moving, like a rocket travelling through space.

NEWTON'S FIRST LAW

Newton's first law states that to make an object go faster or slower, you need a force. This is because its momentum keeps it going at the same speed and in the same direction. If an astronaut pushed himself away from a spacecraft, he could drift off into space forever because there is nothing in space to stop him.

A spacecraft coming back to Earth is travelling very fast, but it relies on friction with the air to slow it down. This is why it gets very hot.

TRAVEL IN SPACE

Moving through space is very different to moving on the ground. When a car moves, its wheels push against the ground. As soon as they stop pushing, friction slows the car down. In empty space, there is nothing to stop a spacecraft moving – but there is nothing to push against either, not even air. So how does a spacecraft move?

Skylab

Space stations only need a little power to keep them in orbit because they are moving through space very fast and so have a lot of momentum.

In space, a rocket is kept going by its own momentum and a few bursts from booster rockets.

The Secret of Space Travel

You can't push unless there's something to push against. Newton's third law shows how, when a force pushes one way, an equal force pushes in the opposite direction. If you throw a ball while on roller skates, you will roll back a little way in reaction as the ball moves forwards. Rockets move through space in the same way. As the burning fuels swell out behind a rocket, they push it forwards in an equal and opposite reaction. When an astronaut opens a hatch in space, her body also turns in an opposite reaction.

NEWTON'S SECOND LAW

The amount something speeds up or slows down – the acceleration – depends on just how strong the force is and how heavy the object is. The heavier a rocket is, the more force it needs to get it into space. A big car is also harder to get moving than a small car.

9

CHAPTER 2 – ROCKET POWER

Some rockets, such as booster rockets, burn a solid rubbery fuel, but most are powered by liquid fuel. Liquid fuel only burns with oxygen, but there is no oxygen far above the ground. So the rocket must also carry a chemical that provides oxygen, called an oxidizer. The fuel and oxidizer mix in a combustion chamber, then a spark called an igniter sets them alight.

Blow up a balloon and let it go. It darts about as it reacts against the air rushing out of it. Rockets work in much the same way.

Ariane V blasts off

LIQUID-FUEL ROCKETS

Different rockets use different fuels – the space shuttle uses liquid hydrogen and Saturn V used kerosene. Most types of fuel are pumped into the combustion chamber with an oxidizer such as liquid oxygen (or LOX). Here they burn together to create a high-pressure stream of gases which roars out through a small nozzle at speeds of about 15,000 km/h.

The nozzle is shaped so that the gases roar out of the rocket at the maximum speed and pressure.

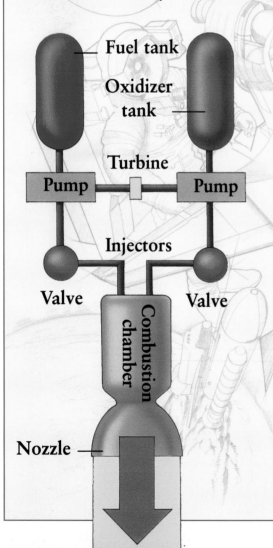

Fuel tank

Oxidizer tank

Turbine

Pump   Pump

Injectors

Valve   Valve

Combustion chamber

Nozzle

Too narrow

Too wide

For the first few minutes of flight, the rocket's speed is limited by gravity and, as it speeds up, friction with the air. As it climbs higher, these get less and less.

As it burns more fuel, the rocket itself gets lighter. Once in space, it only needs a little fuel to keep it going.

Liquid oxygen

Fuel line

Liquid hydrogen

LIQUID FUEL ROCKET

Nozzle

MODEL ROCKET
PART 1
NOZZLE

ADULT HELP NEEDED

1 Find a cork that fits a two-litre drinks bottle. Then ask an adult to drill a hole through it, just wide enough for a valve to fit tightly.

2 Seal the surface of the cork by painting PVA glue over the outside of it. Leave the hole free of glue.

3 When the glue is dry, push the valve through the hole in the cork. Use the same sort of valve you would use to pump up a football or basketball.

ARIANE V

Ariane V

Rocket fuel burns incredibly quickly, and most rockets only have enough fuel to last a few minutes. The main engine in the Ariane V rocket (see page 10) burns for ten minutes. In this time it uses 158 tonnes of fuel.

MMUs

MMU

You don't have to burn rocket fuel to move around in space. Forcing any gas out through a nozzle will provide a push in the opposite direction.

The Manned Manoeuvring Units (MMUs) that astronauts strap on their backs for spacewalks use jets of cold nitrogen gas in this way.

Nozzles pointing in different directions (*right*) move the MMU and steer it in the direction the astronaut wants to go.

OTHER ROCKET ENGINES

In rockets powered with liquid fuels, the fuels weigh an enormous amount and are dangerously explosive. So space engineers have experimented with other engines.

Solid-fuel rockets are already used. But scientists are trying other ideas, including NERVA engines (*below*). These pump hydrogen gas at high pressure into a nuclear reactor. This creates a powerful jet which propels the rocket into space.

Booster

NERVA ENGINE

Bottles pump in hydrogen

Liquid oxygen

Liquid hydrogen

Solid fuel

Once ignited, solid-fuel engines cannot usually be stopped or restarted, so they are generally used for short missions or for small booster rockets that make fine changes to direction.

SOLID-FUEL ROCKETS

Parachutes allow boosters to fall back to Earth

Solid-fuel rocket engines are the oldest of all engines and were used by the Chinese almost a thousand years ago. They are basically rods of solid fuel with a tube down the middle. When the fuel is set alight it burns out through the tube. In the space shuttle, the fuel lasts about two minutes.

Nuclear reactor

Nozzle

A-1 Sputnik Titan 34D CZ-4 Energia — ЭНЕРГИЯ

THE NEW SHUTTLE

If the Venture Star (*below*) is a success, flights into space could be as routine as flights on an aeroplane. With its "linear aerospike" engines – rockets arranged in rows – Venture Star can take off and land again and again, like an aeroplane.

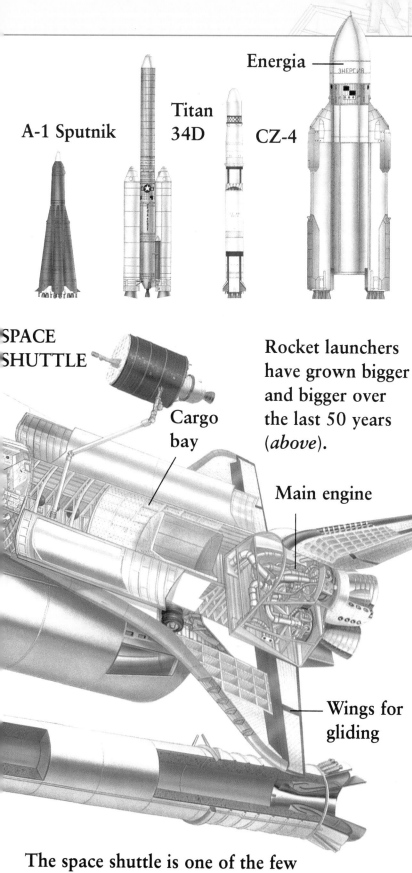

SPACE SHUTTLE

Rocket launchers have grown bigger and bigger over the last 50 years (*above*).

Cargo bay

Main engine

Wings for gliding

The space shuttle is one of the few spacecraft that uses solid-fuel rockets to boost it into space. The shuttle has two solid rocket boosters (SRBs) as well as three main engines, each powered by liquid fuel from a big strap-on tank.

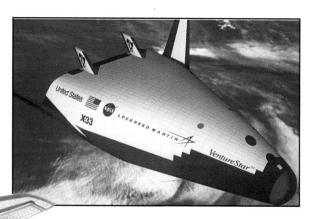

DANGER: EXPLOSIVE!

Scientists do all they can to reduce accidents, but space travel is risky. When a spacecraft takes off on liquid-fuel rockets, it is riding on a giant bomb. In 1986, the space shuttle Challenger (*below*) blew up on lift-off.

Third stage

Nose cone falls away

Satellite

Second stage

Most satellites need to be protected to cope with the force of gravity during lift-off. Some are launched inside the nose cone of the rocket, which falls away just like the booster sections (*left*).

CONSTRUCTION

To cope with the kind of energy needed to thrust a spacecraft high into the sky, rockets have to be incredibly tough. Temperatures in the combustion chamber of a solid-fuel rocket can soar well over 3000° C. Yet rockets have to be light too. So engineers build them from tough, light materials such as titanium.

Boosters

First stage

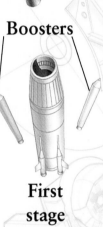

MODEL ROCKET
PART 2
THE BODY & FINS

1 Use the plan at the end of the book to mark out a fin onto balsa wood. Then get an adult to help you cut out four identical fins using a craft knife.

2 Glue the fins to the bottom of a two-litre plastic drinks bottle with strong epoxy glue, so that they form a cross pattern (*right*).

BOOSTER STAGES

The amount of fuel needed to launch most spacecraft is still so huge that most rockets are simply giant fuel tanks. Once a spacecraft has escaped the pull of Earth's gravity, there is no need for all this fuel. So the rockets are built in stages that fall away as the spacecraft climbs higher and fuel is burned up.

LIGHT BUT STRONG

Rockets are built like giant tin cans. It's easy to squeeze a soft drinks can in at the sides. But you'll find it's almost impossible to squeeze it from the ends. This is because the rigid rim of the can spreads the pressure of your squeeze through the length of the can. Rockets are light and strong in the same way.

Space stations that are far too big to launch are put together in space, bit by bit, by astronauts (*above*).

The sides of some rockets are not thick metal sheets but two thin sheets separated by a honeycomb of very thin metal boxes (*right*). This structure is light and strong.

First stage

Second stage

Third stage

SATURN V
ROCKET

Lunar
modules

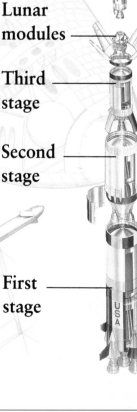

Lunar
modules —

Third
stage

Second
stage

First
stage

SHAPES IN SPACE

On Earth, friction between the air and a vehicle's surface causes drag. This force slows a vehicle down. Out in space, there is no air, and it doesn't really matter what shape a spacecraft is. Probes (*right*) are often awkward shapes, with parts sticking out at all angles.

The Viking probe (*below*) was sent to look for life on Mars.

Spacecraft coming back to Earth have a flat front, so that the air acts as a brake.

Rockets have a pointed nose to slice through the air.

DRAG

Drag is a force that slows moving objects down when a gas or liquid flows past them. You can feel the effect of drag by pulling your hand through a bowl of water.

Viking lander

Solar panels

Fuel tanks

MODEL ROCKET

PART 3

THE NOSE

3 Then glue the nose cone to the base of the drinks bottle – the top of the rocket.

1 Cut out the nose cone shape from card, using the plan at the front of this book.

2 To make the cone, overlap the two straight sides of the nose cone shape and glue them together.

Solar panels catch the Sun's rays and provide probes with energy.

THE PAYLOAD

When a spacecraft takes off, most of its weight is fuel and fuel tanks. The space shuttle weighs only 75 tonnes, but the total weight of the fuel tanks, rockets and fuel needed to blast it into space is 2,000 tonnes. The amount the shuttle can carry in its cargo bay is just 30 tonnes.

a
b
c

The payload is what rockets carry into space, such as (*above*):
a) probe – a spacecraft with no crew
b) mission with human crew
c) satellites

RE-ENTRY

When the wind blows very hard, it can make your face sting. But imagine the force when a shuttle travelling at over 20,000 km/h re-enters the Earth's atmosphere. The friction with the air makes the shuttle very hot. So its nose and underside are coated with heat-resistant ceramic tiles.

During their descent, spacecraft are pulled by gravity like any other object. In the past, small space capsules used parachutes to slow the last bit of their fall (*right*).

Shuttles fly back to Earth under their own power – like an aeroplane.

Too shallow
Correct angle
Too deep

A shuttle must re-enter at the correct angle. If it comes in too shallow, it bounces off the atmosphere; if it aims too deep, it burns up.

CHAPTER 3 – WHAT IS SPACE?

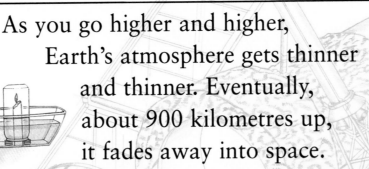

As you go higher and higher, Earth's atmosphere gets thinner and thinner. Eventually, about 900 kilometres up, it fades away into space.

Space is the vast, black emptiness between planets and stars. In space, there is not even air to breathe. But it is constantly crossed by streams of dangerous radiation from the Sun and other stars.

WHERE IT STARTS

It is hard to say where the atmosphere ends and space begins. For astronauts, space starts at 130 kilometres above the Earth, the lowest height a spacecraft can stay in orbit. On the ground you can drive that distance in an hour – so space is not far from the surface of our planet.

The atmosphere only fades off into empty space in a layer called the exosphere. The exosphere is about 775 kilometres above ground.

Gasp!

A portion of air is oxygen, the gas most things, such as rocket fuel, need to burn. But there is no oxygen (or any other gas) in space. To see what happens when oxygen is used up, get an adult to try this experiment.

1 Stand a candle in a shallow bowl of water. The water makes sure no extra air can reach the candle.

2 Light the candle and put a glass jar over it. After a while, the candle goes out. This is because most of the oxygen in the jar has been used up.

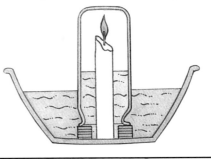

Thermosphere (90–775 km up)
Temp. from -120°C to 2000°C.

Jet

Surface

Sea level – The temperature on the surface is about 11°C.

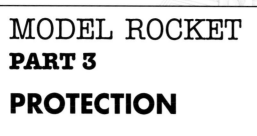

MODEL ROCKET
PART 3
PROTECTION

1 Use acrylic paint to paint the rocket's nose and tail fins. Wrap tin foil around the body of the rocket, with the shiny side facing outwards.

2 Try this experiment to see how spacecraft can be protected in space. Fill two bottles with water. Wrap one in tin foil and paint the other black. Leave them in the sunshine. After an hour, feel each bottle. The bottle wrapped in foil will feel much cooler than the black one, because the Sun's rays bounce off the shiny foil.

Spacesuits stop astronauts from getting too hot or cold. They also shield against the Sun's rays. We are normally protected from these rays by the Earth's atmosphere (but we can get sunburnt).

Shuttle

Stratosphere (13-55 km up)
Temp. from -60° to 10°C.

EARTH

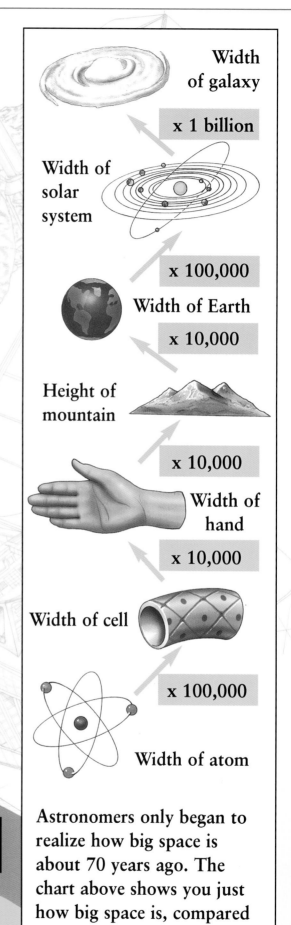

Width of galaxy

x 1 billion

Width of solar system

x 100,000

Width of Earth

x 10,000

Height of mountain

x 10,000

Width of hand

x 10,000

Width of cell

x 100,000

Width of atom

Astronomers only began to realize how big space is about 70 years ago. The chart above shows you just how big space is, compared to things around us.

SATELLITES

Artificial satellites are the 2,000 or so spacecraft that circle the Earth non-stop. They fly round at a height where their speed perfectly matches the pull of Earth's gravity.

They whizz round the Earth just too fast to be pulled down by gravity – yet not so fast that they fly off into space.

Sketch the flight path of a satellite (see page 21).

The Hubble Space Telescope (or HST, *below*) has taken the only accurate pictures of the tiny and distant planet Pluto and has revealed the best evidence for black holes in space.

Radio antenna

SATELLITES

There are many kinds of satellites. Communications satellites, for instance, bounce telephone and radio signals around the world. Weather satellites show the weather from above. In the picture on the left, a satellite is being repaired by astronauts on a space shuttle.

Mirror B

Cylinder

HUBBLE SPACE TELESCOPE

Telescopes in orbit get a clear view of objects in space because there is no atmosphere to affect their view. The most famous is the Hubble Space Telescope. It gathers light in the cylinder, which is reflected by mirror A towards mirror B. This then reflects the image back towards cameras and other scientific instruments.

Mirror A

Instruments and cameras

SATELLITE PATHS

Satellites circle the Earth at different heights above the ground. The highest ones orbit at exactly the same speed as the Earth is turning, so seem to stay in the same place above the Earth. Satellites lower down seem to pass over the surface of the Earth in a wavy path (*right*).

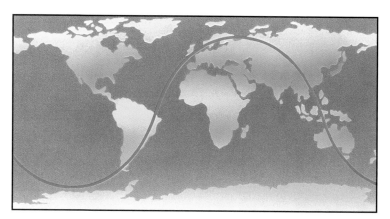

First pass

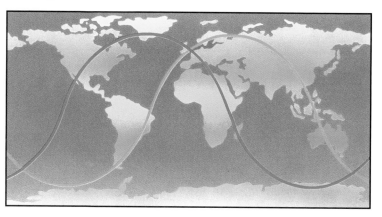

Second pass – path changes as the Earth spins

Solar panels

The HST could spot a coin 640 km away!

Instruments and cameras

It can be tricky to repair a satellite when it is travelling so fast. A shuttle crew must choose exactly the right speed to match the satellite's orbit.

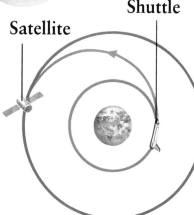

Satellite

Shuttle

Satellite Orbit

Try this experiment to see why satellite paths seem wavy.

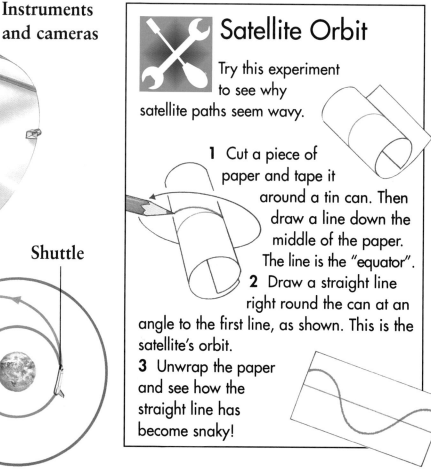

1 Cut a piece of paper and tape it around a tin can. Then draw a line down the middle of the paper. The line is the "equator".

2 Draw a straight line right round the can at an angle to the first line, as shown. This is the satellite's orbit.

3 Unwrap the paper and see how the straight line has become snaky!

To see how satellites turn in space, hold on to a bicycle wheel by the hub and sit on a swivel chair. Get an adult to spin the wheel very rapidly. Try tilting the wheel and you will find that the effect is to swivel you one way or the other on the chair.

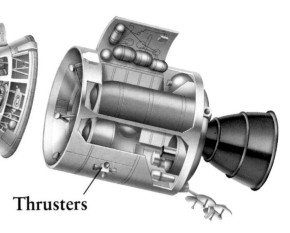

Thrusters

MOVING IN SPACE

Out in space, spacecraft don't have to deal with the powerful pull of Earth's gravity or push their way through the atmosphere. There are, however, still plenty of problems with moving in space – especially for probes that need to turn just a little bit for the right camera angle.

Many spacecraft have a set of thruster rockets. These are small rockets with nozzles pointing in different directions. To change direction, the spacecraft fires particular sets of nozzles.

Probe spins the other way.

Reaction wheel spins one way.

Giotto

Probes such as Giotto and Galileo have gyroscopic systems to control the way they are pointing. These use a heavy spinning wheel called a reaction wheel, like the bicycle wheel on the swivel chair (*top*). When a small motor changes the angle of the reaction wheel, the momentum of the spinning reaction wheel makes the whole probe swivel.

Galileo

SLINGSHOT EFFECT

Many space probes travelling through the solar system use the planets to help them on their way. They fly close enough to a planet to use the pull of its gravity to accelerate them on through space, on a different course. It is a bit like a stone being spun around and hurled from an old-fashioned sling, which is why this is called the slingshot effect.

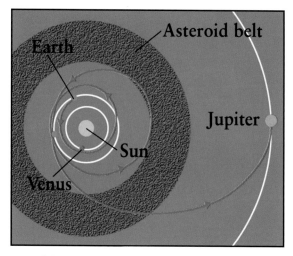

Galileo used Venus and Earth in a "slingshot" towards Jupiter (*above*).

MOON LANDING

When the Apollo space missions landed men on the Moon, the main "command module" stayed circling the Moon in space. The astronauts touched down on the Moon's surface in a small, light "lunar module" little bigger than a caravan. This had its own rockets to let it down slowly and boost it back into space.

Lunar module

Unlike the Moon, Mars has a thick atmosphere. So when the Mars Sojourner landed there in 1997, it could use a parachute to slow its fall. It also inflated its own airbags to soften the landing.

CHAPTER 4 – LIVING IN SPACE

When astronauts travel into space, the spacecraft must not only protect them from the radiation of space; it must also provide all they need in order to breathe, eat, drink and sleep. Once in orbit, the astronauts have to deal with weightlessness. This means that things float freely because gravity does not hold them down.

To run, the equipment on board a spacecraft needs a lot of energy. As well as solar panels (*above*), spacecraft have batteries to store electricity for use when they are in the Earth's shadow.

Port to link up with other spacecraft

Escape capsule

Laboratories

SPACE FOOD

Space food must be healthy and easy to use and store. On early missions, astronauts ate dried and powdered food to which they added water. Now they have ready-meals like microwave meals at home (*above*).

24

When the International Space Station (*below*) is finished, it will be 108 m long and 90 m wide.

It will provide a complete environment for dozens of people to work in space for months at a time.

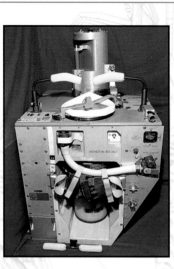

KEEPING A BALANCE

To survive, astronauts need oxygen as well as food and drink (*below*). Machines in spacecraft provide oxygen and remove the carbon dioxide that the astronauts breathe out. Space toilets (*left*) save the water from bodily waste and blast the dry matter into space.

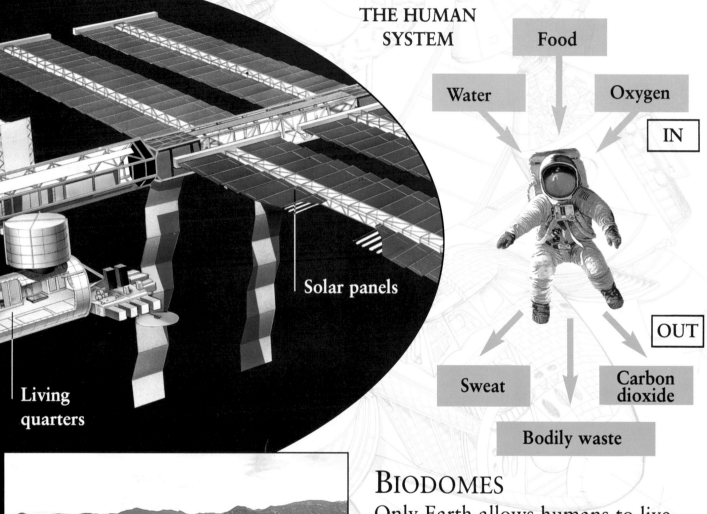

THE HUMAN SYSTEM

Food

Water

Oxygen

IN

OUT

Sweat

Carbon dioxide

Bodily waste

Solar panels

Living quarters

BIODOMES

Only Earth allows humans to live without any protection. If we are ever to live on other planets, it will have to be inside completely sealed buildings (like the Biosphere 2 experiment, *left*) that provide all our needs, just like a spacecraft.

COMMUNICATIONS

The launch

Even when far out in space, astronauts and spacecraft can keep in touch with mission control on the ground in a number of ways. Astronauts talk to mission control by radio. Television pictures are beamed back to Earth. Computers, sensors and other equipment on the spacecraft send back streams of signals via radio waves.

This shuttle cockpit (*above*) shows the huge number of control systems that are needed in a spacecraft.

Sometimes signals can be beamed directly between the space shuttle and mission control.

Shuttle

Relay satellite

MISSION CONTROL

Mission control (*above*) follows every spacecraft constantly, but the link is not always easy to maintain. Sometimes the spacecraft may be out of sight round the other side of the world, or on the far side of a planet. Important messages are often printed out so they can be checked.

When the shuttle is out of sight, sometimes signals have to be bounced off a relay satellite.

Fuel tanks
released

Manoeuvre
for re-entry

Launch satellite

Release boosters

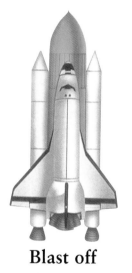

Re-entry

MODEL ROCKET
PART 5
BLAST OFF!

1 Pour about 0.5 litres of water into your rocket and place the cork firmly into the neck of the bottle. Attach a bicycle pump to the valve in the cork and stand the rocket on its fins on a hard surface outside. Pump air into your rocket until it blasts off.

WARNING: DO NOT STAND OVER THE ROCKET AS THE AIR IS PUMPED IN.

2 Find out what level of water gives the best results.

Glides back
to Earth

Blast off

SHUTTLE MISSION

The space shuttle was the first reusable spacecraft. It is often used for carrying satellites into space or repairing them in orbit. It is also used to ferry crew members to and from space stations.

If your car breaks down, you can take it to the garage. In space, it's not quite so easy! When the Mir space station got damaged (*left*), it cost millions of pounds to keep it in orbit. In the end, the station was abandoned.

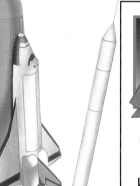

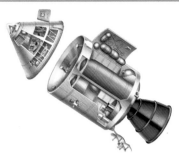

SCIENCE PRINCIPLES

LOOK BACK AND TEST YOUR KNOWLEDGE

NEWTON'S FIRST LAW

Newton First Law of Motion is about changes in movement. It states that whenever something moves – even the least bit differently – there is a force involved. When something starts to move, speeds up, slows down or simply changes direction, there is a force involved. It is all to do with inertia and momentum.

MOMENTUM

Everything that is standing still has inertia. This means it won't move unless something forces it to. Everything that is moving has momentum. This means it won't slow down or speed up unless something forces it too. Something heavy and fast, like a car, has a lot of momentum. It's the car's momentum that crushes it when it crashes into a wall (*above*).

 (1) Why does a shuttle have wings? Answers to all questions on pages 28-29 are on page 32.

NEWTON'S SECOND LAW

Newton's Second Law of Motion is about how effective a force is. The amount something speeds up or slows down is the acceleration. Newton's Second Law states that acceleration depends on how big the force is and how heavy the object is. To throw a heavy ball fast, you need a strong throw.

(2) What do you think falls faster, a bullet or a marble dropped from the same height?

NEWTON'S THIRD LAW

When you walk, the ground pushes up against your feet with the same force. If it didn't, your feet would sink into the ground just like they do into water. If the ground pushed harder, it would fire you into the air.

Whenever anything moves (or is pushed, *above right*), there is always this balance of forces working in opposite reactions.

GRAVITY

Gravity is the natural force that pulls everything together. Every bit of matter in the universe has its own gravitational pull. The strength of the pull depends on just how far apart things are and how big they are – or rather, their mass, which is how much matter they are made of.

Big, heavy objects pull harder than small, light objects. This is why Earth's gravity is strong enough to hold us on the ground, but we can't feel an egg's gravity.

? *(3) Would a full sack feel lighter or heavier as you get further away from the Earth?* (clue above)

RADIATION

Radiation is a spreading of energy. Sometimes you can see it. The light you see things by is a kind of radiation. The world is warm and bright because the Sun radiates light and heat (*below*). Most radiation, though, is invisible, like X-rays and radio waves.

TECHNICAL TERMS

Booster – An additional rocket designed to push the spacecraft further on its journey.

Centrifugal force – A force that seems to throw you outwards when you move in a circle. When a satellite is in orbit, this force is exactly balanced by gravity.

Liquid fuel – Rocket fuel carried in liquid form, such as kerosene.

Manned Manoeuvring Unit – The rocket-powered backpack that moves an astronaut around on spacewalks.

Orbit – A complete circuit around something – often by a satellite or spacecraft held close to a planet by gravity.

Oxidizer – The source of oxygen needed for liquid fuel to burn.

Payload – The items carried into space, such as astronauts and equipment.

Re-entry – The point at which a spacecraft returning to Earth leaves space and enters the Earth's atmosphere. As it does so, friction with the air in Earth's atmosphere makes the spacecraft very hot.

Satellite – Anything that circles another object in space. Moons are natural satellites. Artificial satellites are spacecraft that circle Earth.

Thrust – The "strength" of a rocket engine – that is, how powerfully it pushes.

SPACECRAFT PARTS

There are two main kinds of spacecraft currently in use. First, there is the plane-like space shuttle that carries astronauts into low space orbits. Then there are unmanned spacecraft which carry probes and satellites into space, tucked inside a nose cone.

SPACE SHUTTLE

Two solid-fuel rocket boosters power the shuttle into the air for two minutes after the launch.

1 MAIN ENGINES

These continue after the boosters fall away. They are fuelled by a big external tank.

2 VERTICAL STABILIZER

Like an aeroplane's tail, the vertical stabilizer helps the shuttle to steer.

3 WINGS

The shuttle uses wings to glide through the air after it re-enters the atmosphere.

4 FLIGHT DECK

Two of the crew sit on the flight deck during launch and re-entry. Here they control the shuttle.

5 CARGO BAY

The shuttle has a big cargo bay for carrying objects such as satellites into space. This can be opened without affecting the crew compartments.

WHERE ARE THEY?

Can you guess where pictures A-C were taken? One is on Mars, one is near the Earth and one is on the Moon. Which one is which?

SATURN V

6 FIRST STAGE

The first stage of a rocket is always the biggest, providing the huge thrust needed to push the spacecraft vertically off the ground.

7 SECOND STAGE

Once the first stage has launched the rocket, it burns out and drops away. Then the second stage fires to push the rocket faster and further up.

8 THIRD STAGE

The third stage gives the rocket its final push to a speed where it is free of Earth's gravity.

PAYLOAD

A-C are different kinds of payload carried inside the nose cone of spacecraft. One is for landing astronauts on the Moon, one is a satellite and one is a space probe. Can you guess which is which?

9 OXIDIZER TANK

One tank provides the oxygen the fuel needs to burn (as there is no oxygen in space).

10 FUEL TANK

Another tank provides the fuel that can be burned when it is combined with oxygen.

11 NOSE CONE

Inside the nose are the three spacecraft (*below*) used for a Moon landing.

12 LUNAR MODULE

This takes astronauts down to the Moon's surface.

13 SERVICE MODULE

This circles above the Moon.

14 COMMAND MODULE

This carries the astronauts back to Earth.

INDEX

The finished model rocket

Answers to pages 28–29
1 A shuttle has wings so that it can glide down once it has re-entered Earth's atmosphere. **2** Even though the bullet is travelling faster in a horizontal direction, the marble and the bullet fall at about the same speed. Because they weigh about the same, gravity pulls them down with the same force. **3** The sack would feel lighter the further away from the Earth you get, as the force of gravity gets less.

Answers to page 30
The Moon = **A**, Mars = **B**, Earth = **C**

Answers to page 31
Space probe = **A**, Satellite = **B**, Craft for landing on moon = **C**.

PHOTO CREDITS
Abbreviations – t – top, m – middle, b – bottom, r – right, l – left, c – centre:

Cover and page 13m - Lockheed Martin.
Page 4t, 13b, 17, 24m & 25b - Frank Spooner Pictures.

Page 6, 7 both, 10, 12, 13t, 15, 19, 20, 24b, 25t, 26 all, 27 & 30 all - National Aeronautics and Space Administration (NASA).